BLESSING PEACOCKS

By

Dr.V.P.RATHI

SHANLAX PUBLICATIONS
Madurai, Tamil Nadu, India

BLESSING PEACOCKS

First Edition: 2018

ISBN: 978-93-87102-97-2

Price: Rs.205 /-

Publisher
SHANLAX PUBLICATIONS
61, 66 T.P.K. Main Road
Vasantha Nagar
Madurai – 625003
Tamil Nadu, India

Ph: 0452-4208765,
Mobile: 7639303383
email:publisher@shanlaxpublications.com
web: www.shanlaxpublications.com

FOREWORD

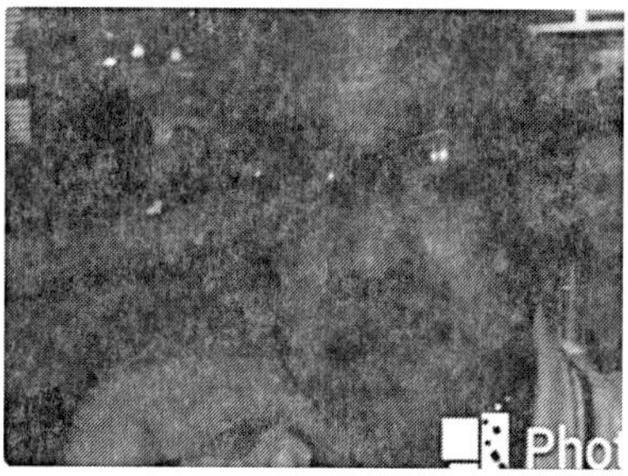

Prof. K. SRIKRISHNAN

Formerly Professor and Head Department of English

Mannar Thirumalai Naicker College, Madurai

Dear VPR - Best Wishes!

V. P. Rathi's avatar as a poet in English is timely and appropriate as she happens to be one of the best students of English Literature always. With her role as an English teacher in Mannar Thirumalai Naicker College under the efficient headship of Dr.A.Arjunan who must have inspired her so well that she has blossomed as an English poet with many characteristics that makes her poems unique. It is a perfect take off-she will indeed soar higher helping her readers too to experience newer feels and vibes of life.

Reading her poems affirm faith in human existence as poetry is the best medium to echo divinity in all its facets. Hope and confidence that she tries to convey through her poems touch our heart with striking imagery and apt feelings. In TIME she points out: "One day time may honour you / Another day Time may corner you" is just an eye opener to any one affected with pride and ego. "Colourful nature which colours my days chanted me Good Morning!" from "Good Morning!" speaks volume of her fertile imagination and the zest for life one must possess each morning.

Her social concern while using a broomstick in **Broomstick Speaks** "Is there any broomstick to obliterate all the caste?" is certainly thought provoking. We appreciate her self confidence and faith when she writes in A to Z poetry (what a title!) "Readiness for all improves your life style"- "Voracious soul discovers God" – these lines appear as revelations of profound truth in simple words. And again in **Inspiration** – "Simplicity never enervates mind" / "Mind is all ever inspired" convey her strong state of mind to speak as a poet with conviction born of self-discipline and hard work. We understand her as she declares: "Unfolded hands of Creator blessed me Good Evening!" No wonder her poems "**My Mother**" and "**Good Morning**" are chosen to find place in the UGC Expression Journal in 2017! She proves her words "And by intelligence one always wears a crown". As one of her former teachers I am proud about her maturity, innovation and clarity expressed in all her poems. I wish all success in all her future endeavours to bring her poems in all print forms. Day is not far off to see her emerge as a great Indian English poet of considerable stature and class.

Wish you all success.

With Regards

Prof. K. SRIKRISHNAN

FOREWORD

Dr. O. RAVI, M.Sc., M.Phil., Ph.D
Controller of Examinations
Madurai Kamaraj University, Palkalai Nagar, Madurai

"Poetry is the spontaneous overflow of powerful feelings: it takes its origin from emotion recollected in tranquillity." This definition of poetry by William Wordsworth echoed in my ears in the college days and now it passes down my memory lane when I read the poetry collection of Dr. V.P. Rathi. Every piece of writing is an expression of emotions and ethos, ideas and ideals, expressions and imaginations, passions and pathos, variety and vitality, which are being immortalised in verses.

The artistic expression, metrical composition and thematic formation of the human mind in emotional and rhythmical language is very well brought out in this volume taking into consideration the trivial to the sublime. The highly commendable 34 poems showcase a selection of the best contemporary poetry dealing with patriotism and familialism, materialism and spiritualism, realism and naturalism and so on.

It gives me immense pleasure to extend my warmest greetings to Dr. V.P. Rathi as she brings out her first volume "Blessing Peacocks". I appreciate wholeheartedly her noble endeavour of educating the eager and young minds by giving a specific purpose, path and plan to their life by painting her poetry by means of words.

It all shows her educational excellence by inspiring students, by building a strong base for life, and making everyone find a right path. I bear witness to this effect in reading her poetry collection. I believe that this poetical work would create a podium for erudite readers to appreciate and admire. Once again, I extend my felicitations to Dr. V. P. Rathi and congratulate and appreciate the gracious effort and assimilation of wide spectrum of knowledge. I wish her more endeavours in the future.

With Regards

Dr. O. RAVI

FOREWORD

Dr. A. ARJUNAN

Associate Professor & Head

Dean of Arts, Mannar Thirumalai Naicker College, Madurai

V. P. Rathi was spotted as an obedient, enthusiastic and highly motivated student in the class room in Mannar campus at the dawn of the New Millennium. Her reverence for her teachers was something special. V.P. Rathi was one among the students who opted for studying English literature. Little did we realise then that she would be destined to become one of my colleagues known as VPR. Her perseverance and dedication has paid her high dividends. The back benchers are usually called 'dreamers, poets, innovators'. But Rathi has broken this myth and proved that even the 'front benchers too can dream and scrapple in poetry'. She used to sit in front row and faithfully take notes.

Born as the biological daughter of Mr. V. Veera Puthira Pandian and Mrs. V. Jeyalakshmi, She is also now a foster child of the Muse. To paraphrase the immortal quote of Pope, We can testify: Rathi scribbled in numbers and the numbers came. The Muse winks only at her darling children. We nod in endorsement to the dictum of the most sensuous bard of the Romantic era,

John Keats: "If poetry comes not as naturally as the leaves to a tree, it had better come not at all." Simple, natural and spontaneous – these are qualities that sum up VPR's poetic collection. In her poem 'My Mother' she breaks in to celebrating all the virtues of an ideal mother. This poem compels us to assume that she is blessed with a very good mother.

Her respect for her teachers is commendable. It is genuine and spontaneous. In her poem **'My Professor, a Mentor'** she waxes eloquently in her adoration of her teachers who have made profound influence on her. In her debut, she has brought in all the subjects which have fascinated her. Poems like **'Youngster's Mobile Phone'** capture the 'mobile maladies' like addiction, distraction. Rathi has graphically painted the agony and longing of a wife trapped in a digital age. The closing line of the poem "Though you delete me, I shall wait for you in Recycle Bin" speaks volume about the unconditional loyalty of a devoted wife. This poetic collection illustrates what the persona is, what she holds dear to her and what she aspires to be. I am not a prophet. But I can tell confidently that Dr. V. P. Rathi will continue to grow up with the passage of time and the posterity will engage with her. I wish her very best in all her endeavours.

With Regards

Dr. A. ARJUNAN

ACKNOWLEDGEMENT

At the outset, I thank God, the Almighty who showered His blessings in every phase of penning this Poetry. Words are inadequate to express My Sense of gratitude to My Husband Mr. M.V. ARUMUGAM and my son A. AKASH KUMAR who were generous to give me adequate space to complete this first volume of Poetry entitled *Blessing Peacocks*.

I express my sincere thanks to My Mother, Mrs. V. Jeyalakshmi, My Father, Mr. V. Veeraputhira Pandian, My Mother-in-Law Mrs. V. Chinnammal, My Father-in-Law, Mr. M. Veeranan, My Brother, Mr. V. Vijay Anand, My Sister, Mrs. P. Sridevi, my K. Priyadharshini and all Kids in our family for their love, kindness and support.

It is a great privilege to record my profound sense of gratitude and thankfulness to all my mentors - Prof. K. Srikrishnan, Prof. B. Sasisekhara Panicker, Prof. N. Rajsekar, Prof. M. Rajalakshmi, Prof. V. Meenakshi, Prof. R. Mangayarkarasi, and Dr. A. Arjunan who are fountain of inspiration.

It is a great privilege to record my profound sense of gratitude and thankfulness to our college President Mr. S. Raja Gopal, our Secretary Mr. M. Vijayaragavan, the Treasurer Mr. L. Govindarajan, Vice-President Mr. R. Jeyaraman and Asst. Secretary, Mr. K. Rajendrababu, our Principal and Professor of Commerce, Dr. S. Nehru and the Director, Prof. R. Raja Govindasamy who have always been my well-wishers. My heartfelt thanks goes to Dr. S. Rukmangathan, Dr. S.P. Subbiah and Dr. P. Kalaichelvi Dr. P. Padmini, Dr. M. R. Chandran, Dr.N. Parimalanayagi, Hindi Pandit Mrs.Chandra Prabha, Mrs. M. Shathi Babu and Dr. Amirtham for their motivation and support.

I register my special gratitude to My Mentor Dr. A. Arjunan, Associate Professor and Head, Department of English, Mannar Thirumalai Naicker College and Dr. O. Ravi, Controller of Examinations and Professor of Mathematics, Madurai Kamaraj University, Madurai and the Poet and Professor K. Srikrishnan.

Finally, I wish to thank all my school teachers, my friends, my colleagues, well-wishers, students and readers.

Dr. V. P. RATHI

CONTENTS

INANIMATE OBJECTS' VOICE

The rotating wings of the Fan do say be cool,
T.V. instructs watching him always not to be fool;
Chasing hands in a Clock remind of time, a Precious,
"Look at the world..." whisper the Windows, conscious;
Reflect before you act advices the Mirror,
Types the Keypad, live without any error.

Glowing Lamp does implore be bright,
Calendar informs be right to up-to-date;
Touch me less, rings Smart mobile,
Use me fewer, laments automobile;
Roof does shout Aim High, and at last
Prophesies the door... push me hard to achieve goal.

MY INDIA

My India,

A Pluri-racial country, this a multi-lingual isle,

My India an agricultural land, this a multi-media world,

A rich land of natural beauty and soil of duty;

A Subcontinent of massive masculine and feminine beauty,

A purgatory world, and this even other paradise,

An abode of Gods and multi-religions,

His Blessed land, a book of philosophical verse,

An example of platonic love and epitome of Spiritual love,

Glittering emerald seat in the sapphire sea,

A Sage Land of Spiritual Masters!

My India! Rich in cultural oasis,

My motherland, this teeming womb of

Sound writers and orators,

And this spirit inspires the life and literature of all countries

Made me My India and in me My India! My India!

CROWN OF MAN

Honoured is he who wears a crown of tolerance
Heart of a real person is fearlessness,
Apply truth on lips, the best lipstick in the world
Draw an eyelash of confidence around eyes,
Remove the dirt of frailty
Well dress with an apron of honesty
Apply the powder of simplicity.

Build around you a castle of patience
And let in a breeze of obeisance
Sniff and spread everywhere an air of continence
Learn and seize the minute of affection
Shake your daze by meditating condign concentration
Make your days full of satisfaction
So that your life may become adulation!

TREE OF EMERALD

As an emerald tree I shine blissfully
When I beget ripened sons and daughters;
As a magnanimous King I feel proudly
When a hungry man does slaughter and
swallow my lovable children;
As a producer of oxygen I would be happy
When two hundred men inhale my exhale;
As a blessed one I would be satisfied
When a hermit does meditate under my shade;
As a fluttering angel I would be dancing
When my wind-friend does caress me;
As a pleasant-giver I would be kind
When my blossoming crown resolves to carry its fragrance;
As a helper for flowery rain I would be thanking
When my sun-father's rays fall upon me;
As a scapegoat I would be moaning
When an insensitive man beheads me with a scythe.

DEAR GOD

I behold you as dawn but you disappeared soon,
I heard your sweet voice for a while but it flew away a mile,
You are my pleasure when I am in displeasure;
Our future is an unreadable book where You only can look.

Words emitted by others make me to fear and my heart to tear,
But Your word consoles me and pours a honey;
Grief not survives me when Your rays bound me,
Remembrance of Your Honest Countenance
Induces me to do saccharine work.

Among sardonic people, You did sangfroid and
Made me Majestic,
Even at my inclement period, You inclined me for upliftment;
You filled me with a cup of Sun beam when I fed dark,
And You replete with a glass of Moon beam when I am hot.

Oh, My dear God! Grateful to you always I am
When I did feel not proud of me I !

TIME SPEAKS

One day Time may honour you,
Another day Time may corner you;
Time speaks, "Always I am a God of Balance"
But people never maintain a fine balance;
I oscillate between hope and despair for an imbalanced man
At the same time, I am a blessed God for a punctual man;
I am a winner of no beginning and end
But a man who conquers me has a good beginning and end.

At the time of birth, you look at me for horoscope;
But at the time of death, you scold me without any scope;
For a man of thinking, I run slowly with
My little babies minutes and seconds
For a man of action, I run steadily by holding their hands.

Presence of mind treats me perfect,
Conscious mind calls me correct,
Subconscious mind shouts at me incorrect,
Unconscious mind babbles and throws me indirect,
But my judgement on those minds remains direct.

You call me good morning, afternoon,
Evening and sweet of night,
But I pass away soon with a heart of light flight;
You address me by numbers – one, two, three, four, five, etc.,
But I number your address on this earth – who, whom, etc.
I say unto you:
Be relaxed at tea time,
Don't be tensed at exam time,
Enjoy yourself at jolly time,
Prepare yourself for the present time.

MY MOTHER

Darkness, darkness, darkness everywhere
Stored this ugly caterpillar in your womb
I fluttered out as a butterfly when you pained deeply
Oh! Light giver, life-giver, and real caretaker;
A bird of blessings and smile of tender

Thou art the angel of selflessness
And ye are an epitome of forgiveness
"Keeping together" is the only aphorism
Held me close in your bosom,
Whispers love, murmurs love, laments love, lovable to adore.

Your hands did caress me when I moan
How many glasses of tear drops you shed? -
To quench my thirst
Served me with millions of satisfied dishes
Provided food with innumerable spoons of love

As a teacher you taught me letters
As a doctor you treated my illness
As an engineer you did construct my behaviours
As a philanthropist you offered me needed things
As a philosopher you advised me

As a policeman you safeguarded me
As a maidservant you rendered all services
Oh stream of Love, having all hues of human kindness

As a glass of water, you quenched my parching lips
As a cup of tea you boosted me with instant energy
As a bee painstakingly collected and gathered honey
As a bed of roses you rocked me to sleep
As the earth you revolved around me
As a Queen you indicated me the right path
How many incarnations a day?
How many professions in this generation?
Being a worst sufferer, removed all my sufferings
Being the best worker, thou art a peerless God
You sweated to sweeten my life
What shall be my offerings to you?
A bow at the lotus feet of this Divine Mother.

RAIN, RAIN POUR HERE

Rain, rain, pour here
All, we dying of fear
We are poor hear
Sand drops even dry tear

Rain, rain, pour here
Hands of trees longing for you
Parched plants stab itself missing you
Thirsty roots do become crispy
Hot, hot, hot, it's so hot and chilly
Soil tears its skin here and there
Rashes, sores, holes everywhere

Rain, rain, pour here
Clouds thyself cover with water robe
Unfold it as we need of water globe
Drench all waterless lakes
Saturate all gulping ponds
Fill to the banks of rivers,
Roll, roll, roll down to the gravels

Rain, rain, pour here

Cool this scorching earth with marvels.

Nature uncommon with your nonappearance

Rain, rain, rain with your disappearance -

Land is vain, pained, chained and tainted.

GOOD MORNING!

Smiling petals of fragrant flowers lisped me Good morning!
Smoothly flowing whiter falls uttered me Good morning!
Shining sunrays that erases dark night pronounced me
Good morning!
Glittering green painted grasses whispered me Good morning!
Black and white grazing cattle lowed me Good morning!
Floating foams in the sky addressed me Good morning!
Bending branches to shower blessings articulated me Good morning!

Tranquil lake of cool water wished me Good morning!
Gentle breeze touching my cheek softly kissed me Good morning!
Ebb and flow of hungry waves roared me Good morning!
Glimmering soil of smelling emanated all Good morning!
Brown brother of growing mountain expressed me Good morning!
Hither and thither honey butterfly murmured me Good morning!
Colourful nature which colours my days chanted me Good morning!
All nature, pasture creature I replied Good morning!

BROOMSTICK SPEAKS

Oh Mankind! Could you hear my voice?

Whenever floor is dressed up with dust, I deterge the dirty;
Whoever strangles my neck, bow, bend and stoop I
Not to conquer but to sweep away the negatives,
Though I wallow in the dust, I am detached to it.

Many embellishing places and rooms here
But I prefer to stay only at the corner
By holding the position of centre,
Nobody can live far better!

Every day, I am ardent to begin my old job
I felt never bored; yes, I concentrate on my new-old job
Have I ever heaped the valuable things?
But I like to throw the rubbish heaped by you!

I advert, don't care about your reputation
You ought to be careful to do your obligation
Running behind lust, anger, and greed –
All the filthy matters
Man himself becomes a tag-rag!

By piling all wealth in paraphernalia
Earth sweeps away such men and does swallow
Proud I to compare myself to earth
Since earth cleans and rejuvenates itself!

Oh, Mankind! Answer my questions...
Is there any broom to immaculate the stained mind?
Is there any broom to root out humankind to be kind?
Is there any broom to annihilate the idle creature?
Is there any broom to clean ozone layer?

Is there any broom to purify the immodest?
Is there any broom to obliterate all the caste?
Is there any broom to stamp out slavery?
Is there any broom to wipe out bribery?

Is there any broom to eradicate social evils?
Is there any broom to eliminate all stress?
Is there any broom to erase all immoral paths?
Oh dear mankind, please invent some new brooms

Tell me, tell me... I shall wait at the corner.

AN INDIAN ENGLISH TEACHER

As a Woman I may be weak
But as an Indian English Teacher I would attain peak;
In my hope I may not be lame
But of my laziness I would feel shame;
As a paper weight I may support the sheet of perseverance
But as a bobbin I would unroll the bundle of fearlessness.

As a seeker of God I may unlock the wisdom clip
And I comb my hair of knowledge with adorned tulip;
As a role model I may wear a saree of honesty
And as a charity spoon I would feed the sense of dignity.

PHILOSOPHY OF WORDS

Articulate sweet words even at bitter time
Chisel out insulting terms to hear better chime;
Shake it off deceptive words to harmonize
Merge complex words to become unionize;

Fair words enlarge the circle of friendship
Venom words disperse the fellowship;
Spiteful words corrode one's happy mood
Saccharine terms diffuse jolly mood;

Garrulous mouth makes constant trouble
Right laconic speech provides lovable in double;
Perished words cannot bring back life
Imperishable words may arouse strife;

Timing words reveal your personal wit
Tempest words disclose you to be unfit;
Remember, words may sell you
Forget not, words may also buy you;

Affectionate words can even sell a neem leaf
But bitter words can't even sell a banana leaf;
Discharge knowledgeable words to heeding ears
Spray commanding words to the deafened ears;

Mine words from the depth of your mind
Cut out pessimistic words from surface of your thought bind;
I am born and abode only at human mind
So use me meticulously, depart only a word of kind.

A-Z POETRY

Access to the person in a polite way
Bang-on with your preparations henceforth no problems
Candour speech is welcomed by all
Dispense wisdom to all the innocent people
Ebullient action leads to multiple ecstasies
Fair-minded self begins a day of good hope
Gaily face paints happiness around others too
Holistic approach gains one's health
Indefatigable spirit helps the needy
Jocular man renounces unhappiness
Knock out the failures as your rival
Lessen your tension when there is a crisis
Man-management is the most skillful job
Navigate your obstacle and proceed carefully
Obliterate your pessimistic ideas
Pacify your enemies and succeed them
Quest for truth throughout your life
Readiness for all improves your lifestyle
Sagacity person never commits mistakes
Tamed mind chariots controlling over six senses
Undisguised personality reveals friendliness

Voracious soul discovers God

Well-groomed glorifies Cleanliness

X-ray thyself to know who you are

Yearn for liberation from this materialistic world

Zenith is the only attainment for your career.

INSPIRATION

Inspiration blows to scribble a poem
Poem speaks through many attempts
Attempts bring happiness
Happiness leads to renaissance
Renaissance kindles quest
Quest for self craves Power
Power makes supremacy
Supremacy generates hatred.

Hatred brings evil
Evil tests tolerance
Tolerance exposes unbiased
Unbiased personality formulates simplicity
Simplicity never enervates mind
Mind is all ever inspired.

HOPE – A POWERFUL MEDICINE!

Man wishes for miracles to happen
Miraculously could not he bear misfortune?
Always he asketh for rays of luck from Heavenly Sky
But he not realizes heaven in his mind – Why?
Hope, a powerful medicine for the wounded mind
Apply some puff of hopeful dreams around waking thoughts

Look at the energy of Swami Vivekananda,
The spirit of Jhansi Rani with her born child,
The courage of Bhagat Singh before hanging
Behold the sparkling eyes of Mangal Pandey
Customs of Gandhiji's Non-violence
Recall the couplets of Thiruvalluvar
Resurrection of Christ after crucifixion
The Prime dreams of Abdul Kalam,
Give not your hope, the powerful medicine!

BABY

A newly born pearl!
From the shell of mother's womb
The whiny-cry like the chirp of bird,
The soft-petal fingers do hold its mother
Which does seem to be His gentle touch of Lamb?

Sitting on the lap of mother like a waterfall on the lap of river,
The crispy lisp of the baby even melts the heart of harder,
Glittering and twittering eyes like the twinkling stars,
Fluttering hands like the swaying branches,
Tottering legs like rolling waters encircling rock;
Its screeching voice, more than the music of orchestra,
Its spirited dance, greater than trepidations of earth!

Its face does teach delight,
Its words do instruct polite,
Its sleep does signify patient
And utmost, this earthly paradise,
A Little god painted in the hands!

A SUMMER DAY

The enthusiastic morning does fold the hands of sleeping night,
Aged morning steps into bright affluent afternoon,
Relaxed and prolonged afternoon pesters all creatures;
All blessed souls welcome the ephemeral dusk,
The pauper breeze publicizes its amicable mood,
And remembrance of the day is pedalled by sweating night.

MY LIFE PARTNER

Part of my heart united after 24 years
A bouquet of love showered on me
Preserved this Queen by this King of Action
Shared my life and honoured my thoughts
When I shiver, he covered me as a summer
A tamed cloud carried me to right destination
Refilled this pen before it is emptied

Weaves my courage to establish name
Stitches the world lips to embellish fame
Sacrificed his hours to elevate my power
Built in him a beautiful tower
Painted my face with brightness
By educating my mind with kindness
This swan smoothly drifted
But under his restless pedalling

I pray unto God, if I have another birth
Boon the same life after death

YOUNGSTER'S MOBILE PHONE

Modern youngsters wake up at the face of colourful handset
And the day ends at the rest of handset
The Art of reading messages and sending messages
And including deleting messages make a man literate
But the Art of Language does destroy;
Here, New Art of Transliteration is invented.
Typically, Tamil is typed in English and vice versa.
By the way, orthography is tainted into cacography;
Calligraphers decrease in number.

Melodious plot of caller's tune varies one by one of ringing tone
Vibration does lead to tympanic membranes destruction
Learner's dictionary and textonym sleep inside the cell phone;
The talent of the user is buried inside the keypad.

Switching off mobile phone brightens the youngsters,
Silence of the mobile phone is not violence
Remaining a slave, Mobile masters and humanity dies
By mastering the smart phone, humanity lives.

SMILE FOREVER

It relaxes twenty muscles for smiling
And contracts forty for frowning,
What do you prefer – Smiling or Frowning?
Let your lips smile for others
And sorrows flew away from hearts.

Oh Smile!
Aren't you the blazing of the Sun?
Or blossoming of the flower at top mountain?
Are you the gushing of the water after rain?
Put on a smile and start your work,
Otherwise Work does smile and makes to jerk;

The earth smiles when the first rain drop touches
The wind smiles when it does caress the flowers;
The flower smiles when its fragrance reaches others
The twinkling star smiles when darkness appears,
The sun smiles seeing the early riser,
Smile, Smile, Smile, Smile forever.
No need to travel a mile for a smile
Extending half-an-inch on the lips
Makes your life to live such a long journey
And the smile may change your signature an autograph
And life with your pretty smile, a honey.

VOICES OF THE RAIN

Blessed clouds beget me pure,
But I wallow in the dust sure;
I did pass many traditional ages
Whereas living beings do get cure

Priest does admire me - am I holy?
Plants do absorb me - am I Pepsi?
Washer men use and cast me away - am I dirty?
When I am born Peacock dances - am I beauty?

Hail to thee Sun! The Holy Father,
Hail to thee Trees! My sisters,
Hail to thee Oceans! My relatives,
Hail to thee rivers and tributaries! My daughters and sons!

LAMENTATION OF A WIFE IN THE DIGITAL AGE

Am I a Google.com to many?
Anyway you can download online & offline app any!
Daily, daily, my lovable life partner excavates smile app,
Emptying three GB of Smile within me
And dumping eight GB of scolding me;
Connected to me whenever you needed service,
What is up? What is up? I expected your whatsapp
But disconnected me, though net is available!
You clicked on Ctrl + F only to insult me
You pressed Ctrl + E only to blame me
You clicked Ctrl + L only to neglect me
You did long press down arrow key only to pull down me.
You touched all the keys but never exclamation mark
Why? Why do you kick me into the trash?
After all work is done, you did delete this important File,
Though you delete me I shall wait for you in Recycle Bin.

BIRD OF MUSIC

I worship thee bird! Thou art a composer of melodies
To pen poetry, I hunt for words
By reading and re-reading it pains me pouring a word
Bird of lightsome, which books do you read?

Who trained you musical notes?
Thou art the master of Music!
I strain to collect musical instruments,
To generate music have I to learn by academics?

This scholarly bird without paper, pen, books
Creates, composes, compiles....
Songs of Bird neither recorded nor published,
Nor does it expect garland after singing

The timid bird does show not its face
It hides among the leaves of the boughs
But I want to show my face even for simple triumphs
Bird of Music, singing without any words!
Singing poetry through wind,
Playing without any instrument – of music
I marvel this awesome bird!

GOOD EVENING!

Fanning breeze I lisp you Good evening!
Flying daylight I wish you Good evening!
Walking angels I greet you Good evening!
Solo white stone getting ready for procession Good evening!
Singing birds returning home Good evening!
Black blankets of stars covering the earth Good evening!
Nest which welcomes the birds I chirp you Good evening!
Frozen mountains I echo you Good evening!
Colour changing immortal sky I murmur Good evening!
Diminishing, floating shapeless white paper Good evening!
Waking dreams I babble you Good evening!
Unfolded hands of Creator blessed me Good evening!

EDUCATION

For imaginary students, school, a swimming pool
To waste worthy water;
For dunce students, a well to be stagnant entire;
For enthusiastic students, a reservoir how to use it later.

When the buds learn, Fruitful flowers are grown,
The flower emanates the scent of knowledge to be known,
And powered by intelligence one always wears a crown.

To expand your vocabulary, access with Dictionary
To encompass the full range of world, read History
To know the every aspect of human life, trust Biology
To take a tour of the world, win map through Geography
To learn a wealth of information, practice technology
Speech without shy does show your endeavour in Literature
Full installation of colour technology, be ready with Computer

Being educated -
Eradicate the other,
Interrogate the sinner,
Advice the younger.

SHOWER ME, ANGELS!

Angels, Angels, listen to my words –
Is my sleep necessary to awake?
If so ever, shower dreams!
Is my loneliness necessary to think?
If so ever, shower leisure!
Is my profession necessary to earn?
If so ever, shower me ceaseless energy!
Is my writing compulsory to read?
If so ever, shower imaginations!
Is my prayer necessary to God?
If so ever, shower meditation!
Is my death necessary after this life?
If so ever liberate this soul!

Angels, Angels did you heed?
Thus, if thou do as I plead –
Shower Mercy on me!

LADY MACBETH

Lady Macbeth, the wife of Macbeth!
Much I awe this ungainly sculpture
Who deftly chiselled a man of valour;
Powers his mind with capsules of advice
Without the knowledge of panacea for vice;
The undaunted soul does posses manhood
Glorifying her husband, not her nationhood;
Eternal peace nor she achieves in realism
Instead mental conflict leads to somnambulism;
In morbid position bathes her hands unintentionally
Recollecting the gory details of the past wistfully;
Invisible spirit of darkness clouded this woman of temptation
Is there any one to question her fate of aberration?
This energetic shadow echoes vague dissatisfaction;
Illusion leads her gradually to a tragic conclusion
Death clears her path of tangled complication.
Her split-self arouses a tinge of pity
Reading her, we admire Shakespeare's creativity.

MY PROFESSOR, A MENTOR

Fragrance of those teaching days, I remember now
Nurturing and caring for us many a times,
Recharged this battery with immediate knowledge
Spooned with infinite seeking information

Sowed inspiring words, enchanted us thousands of times
Amended our providences, chiselled our Englishes...
Thou art a tree to shelter these ignorant birds,
Birds of your kind learn to fly with intelligible wings.

Though you retire, the roots of thy teaching never cut off
Leaves which pronounced thy valuable lecture never shed off;
Buds that inhale your thoughts, blossom intellectually
Let us consider thy face value, to celebrate thy individuality

A rain of knowledge! Watered this plant with wisdom
A massive key of veracity! Opened our mind of paucity
Thou art Sun! Shine we, Full moon with your reflections.
What shall be our offerings? O beloved Progenitor!
Promise I here... to generate education to my Offspring!

SMART PHONE – A FIFTH RENAISSANCE

Reading & Writing as an art...
Is it not the first Renaissance?
Joys of Drama, on stage performance...
Is it not the second Renaissance?
Novelty of reading novels, watching movies...
Is it not the third Renaissance?
By computer, laptop, a revival of art and literature...
Is it not the fourth Renaissance?
Smart phone, tab do millisecond research!
Is it not the fifth Renaissance?

World shrinks small to small, in our hands...
We come to know foot to hat, bit to hit, second to second,
Time to time, place to place a power of infinity!
Unearthing history, philosophy, science, geography...

Butterfly casket! Carried as baby in hands
Feeds us knowledge, spreads news...
An eye-opener to professional to non-professional
Thiruvalluvar, Socrates, Will Durant, Confucius, Bruce Lee,
Shakespeare, Emerson, Freud, Hirohito, Lenin,...
Plenty of book learning, uncovering their phases and faces

All manuscripts, printed forms organised in details

Long written work, short written work

Bound together from great book to face book

People blessed twice and thrice by this magic renaissance.

WELCOME TO MADURAI CITY...

Welcome to splendid, sleepless city,
Not to spend unawakened day
But to rouse your cloudy, hazy thought
Filled with monuments, towers, lakes,
This City of food provides tainty food,
Dear all, Welcome to Madurai City...

The slang of Madurai never ruins its language
Unique vocabulary borrowed by many
A blithesome nature pleases every one
Hearty melodious songs originated here
Words of wisdom scattered here
Dear all, Welcome to Madurai City...

Manifestations of strength seen among men and women
Showing tenderness, the heart of people
Hardly could find annoying person
Beaten Literary genres by creative pens
A reflection on this city impacted screen writers
Dear all, Welcome to Madurai City...

A dwelling place of confidence to daily bread wagers
Overworked business men return home tireless

Moving towards clockwise is the path of office-goers;
Practicing a Profession, the motto of educational institutions
Birds and animals, good comrades treated chiefly
Dear all, Welcome to Madurai City...

Marks in the annals of World History, awesome!
The land bequeaths gardens of Jasmines that blossom;
The voices of Madurai echo in our hearts
A past and present City of Culture and Venture
This city of Temple shields us from catastrophe,
Rain of memories marks memoirs in each psyche.
Dear all, Welcome to Madurai City...

PENNING POETRY

Ear fails to hear while inner voice ringing
Fail eyes to see while imagining
No taste to tongue while word consuming
Thirst no to throat while pronouncing
Action no to body while fingers scribbling
No air to breathe while thought inhaling
Heart speaks only while message conveying
Ha, ha, ha this is what penning poetry.

INDUSTRIOUS NATURE

Formless foam, why do you tremble?
Have you become reeling white man?

Fearless tree, after growing, why do you lisp?
Have you become child?

Ageless mountain, serious looking, why do you peep?
Have you become complan boy?

Rust-less river, ceaseless runner, why do you chase?
Have you become policeman?

Colourless moon, floating tablet, why do you wane/wax?
Have you become celebrity?

Imaginary blue sheet, why do you spread?
Have you become propagandist?

Revolving blue planet, why do you spin?
Have you become cyclist?

Industrious nature, why do you work?
Have you become Bustling worker?

MY FATHER

My Father,
An epistle posted by your dear daughter
A great orator who taught me little words
Cultivated me by your majestic thoughts,
Motivated me when I am dejected,
Accelerated my success when I stepped ahead,

Oh Pathmaker!
Travelled, trotted, left an indelible mark!
I am here to follow your foot trace,
Not to compete as a kind of race...
For a spoon of rice, you perspired for hours,
Surrendered your wealth at the speed of thy strength

Oh My Shepherd!
Thou art an adroit leader
Who did handle problems with care
Your honesty reflected in my every day activity,
Your simplicity awakened my spirituality.
Thy name is embossed in my heart for thy generosity.

Oh My Noble hero!

I walked on with your shadows of familiarity,
Though time spent little with you...
That's the greater time of mine.
Before dispatching this letter
I end this missive with your initials.

BUTTERFLIES

Butterflies, butterflies, Queen of flies, flies, flies,
Of yellow black, black golden, golden brown, brown green!
Painted with all hues, painted with all hues?
The Big Hand who dipped the brush in Sky-clouds
Made you blue and white, blue and white! Blue and white!
He who touched the Sun and made you golden?
Golden, golden, and yellow golden!
Wallowing the brush in the muddy soil and
Made you brown, made you brown!
He touched the Sky-dark and applied black
Made you black, made you black, black!
Who sprinkled white little, little moons on you?
Little moons, little moons, on you?
Show me the Colour boxes of Nature that He used,
Show me the Gigantic Hands who applied microscopic level!
With thou lightest wings, of heaviest hands!
Emptied my mind and filled with joy,
Joyous, marvellous, adventurous, adventurous!
Butterflies, butterflies, Queen of flies, flies, flies...